The Flavours Series

PEACHES, PEARS & PLUMS

ELAINE ELLIOT

Photography by Julian Beveridge

FORMAC PUBLISHING COMPANY LIMITED
HALIFAX 1999

PHOTO CREDITS:
All photographs by Julian Beveridge except where noted below:
Dr. Neil Miles, University of Guelph, Department of Plant Agriculture: p 4, top; p 5 top & bottom

PARTICIPATING ESTABLISHMENTS:
Arbor View Inn, Lunenburg, NS
Blomidon Inn, Wolfville, NS
The Briars Resort, Jackson's Point, ON
Catherine McKinnon's Spot O' Tea
  Restaurant, Stanley Bridge, PEI
Charlotte Lane Café & Crafts, Shelburne, NS
Dalvay-by-the-Sea, Dalvay, PEI
The Dundee Arms Hotel, Charlottetown, PEI
The Dunes Café, Brackley Beach, PEI
Home Port Historic Inn, Saint John, NB
Hotel Newfoundland, St. John's, NFLD
Inn at Bay Fortune, Bay Fortune, PEI
Jubilee Cottage Country Inn, Wallace, NS

Kaulback House Historic Inn, Lunenburg, NS
Keltic Lodge, Ingonish Beach, NS
La Maison Dining Room, Halifax, NS
La Perla Dining Room, Dartmouth, NS
Les Fougères Restaurant, Chelsea, PQ
Libertine Café & Kitchen, Halifax, NS
Murray Manor Bed & Breakfast,
  Yarmouth, NS
The Normaway Inn, Margaree Valley, NS
Shadow Lawn Inn, Rothesay, NB
Tattingstone Inn, Wolfville, NS
The Whitman Inn, Kempt, NS
Wickwire House, Kentville, NS

This book is dedicated to the many chefs and innkeepers who have generously provided recipes and support and to my patient family.

Formac Publishing Company acknowledges the support of the Department of Canadian Heritage and the Nova Scotia Department of Education and Culture in the development of writing and publishing in Canada.

Canadian Cataloguing in Publication Data
Elliot, Elaine, 1939-
    Peaches, Pears and Plums
    (The Flavours series)
    Includes index.
    ISBN 0-88780-471-3
1. Cookery (Peaches).   2. Cookery (Pears)   3. Cookery (Plums)   I. Title.
II. Series
TX813.P4E44 1999   641.6'413   C99-950062-7

Formac Publishing Company Limited
5502 Atlantic Street
Halifax, N.S.
B3H 1G4

Distribution in the United States:
Seven Hills Book Distributors
1531 Tremont Street
Cincinnati, OH 45214

CONTENTS

INTRODUCTION

$\mathcal{L}$overs of fresh fruit will welcome this latest addition to the Flavours series. It's an exploration of the versatility and delights of peaches, pears and plums. Each fruit has its own characteristics and, although peaches are the heralds of summer, they are followed shortly by plums and pears. With great gusto our chefs prepare delightfully different dishes with these beautiful fruits! From jams and chutneys to salads, main course entrées and desserts, they have shared their personal favourite recipes and I thank them.

Photographer Julian Beveridge has visited many of the dining rooms, capturing the dishes as they are served, thus allowing even a novice cook the chance to "cook inn" and recreate these magnificent dishes. Each recipe has been tested and adjusted to serve four to six persons.

PEACHES

First found in China, the peach tree came to North America via Persia and Europe. The velvety skin of the fruit can vary from pale yellow to deeper hues of gold with a rosy blush. Peaches are very tender and must be picked and handled with care. When purchasing, look for ripe but firm fruit which exude a strong aroma. Avoid soft spots, blemished skin or signs of greening. Under ripe peaches will ripen if stored in a paper bag at room temperature for two to three days. Store ripe fruit in plastic bags in the refrigerator for no longer than five days. Bring fruit back to room temperature before eating. While the fuzzy skin of a peach is edible and full of nutrients, many prefer to peel the fruit before eating. The simplest way to peel a peach is to blanch it in boiling water for 30 seconds and slip off the skin. A 4-ounce serving of unsweetened peach contains 49 calories and is a source of potassium and vitamins A and C.

PEARS

Pears are native to Asia Minor, yet today thousands of varieties are grown in temperate climates throughout the world. The ripe fruit, with skin of green, golden yellow or red blush colour, is juicy and sweet. Pears are best harvested when underripe. Look for slightly firm fruit with unblemished skin. Store at room temperature for a few days to ripen, then refrigerate and use within a few days. Popular varities include Anjou, Bartlett, Bosc and Comice. A 4-ounce serving of unsweetened pear contains 67 calories and is a source of vitamin C and potassium.

PLUMS

Originating in Asia, plums have become a popular fruit in North America. They range in colour from green to red, and from purple to black. Choose plums that are slightly firm to the touch and feel heavy. It is common for plum skin to have a grey film or coating, but avoid fruit with blemishes. Plums will ripen stored at room temperature, and once ripe may be refrigerated in a plastic bag for up to 4 days. Popular varities include Santa Rosa, Red Beauty and Friar. A 4-ounce serving of unsweetened plums contains 63 calories and is a source of potassium and vitamins A and C.

BREAKFAST FARE

The chefs of the many inns and restaurants, who are the source for these recipes, have an amazing repertoire. In this section you will find simple-to-make jams that gel without the addition of commercial pectins, plus delightful dishes prepared for leisurely, elegant breakfasts.

◀ *Warm from the oven, Peaches and Almond Scones served at Home Port Historic Inn, Saint John, NB*

PEACH AND ALMOND SCONES

HOME PORT HISTORIC INN, SAINT JOHN, NB

The Home Port Historic Inn is an elegant establishment perched high on a hill overlooking the busy harbour of Saint John. Innkeeper Ralph Holyoke offers his breakfast guests these scones which he feels are best served right out of the oven.

2 cups flour

1/4 cup sugar

2 teaspoons baking powder

1/2 teaspoon baking soda

1/2 teaspoon salt

1/4 cup butter

1 full cup finely diced peach pieces

1/4 cup almond slivers

1 cup coffee cream (18% m.f.)

1 egg yolk

1/2 teaspoon almond extract

3-4 tablespoons white vinegar

1 egg white, lightly beaten

2 tablespoons sugar

Preheat oven to 400°F.

In a large bowl combine flour, sugar, baking powder, baking soda and salt. Using a pastry blender, cut in butter until mixture resembles coarse crumbs. Stir in peach pieces and almond slivers.

In a separate bowl, blend together cream, egg yolk, almond extract and vinegar. Slowly add the cream mixture to the flour mixture, mixing only until just combined.

Turn out on to a floured pastry board and knead just long enough to form a ball. Do not over work the dough. Flatten the ball and brush with beaten egg white, then sprinkle with sugar.

Cut into wedges and transfer to a greased baking sheet. Bake until golden, approximately 13–15 minutes.

Yields 10–12 wedges.

PLUM JAM

3 cups pitted and finely chopped plums

1/3 cup sugar

1/3 cup water

2 tablespoons fresh lemon juice

2 tablespoons liquid honey.

In a large saucepan, bring plums, sugar and water to a boil. Reduce heat and simmer fruit, stirring frequently, until thickened, approximately 15 minutes.

Remove from heat and stir in honey. Cool, then refrigerate up to 2 weeks. Yields 3 cups.

MURRAY MANOR PEACH JAM

MURRAY MANOR BED AND BREAKFAST, YARMOUTH, NS

At Murray Manor innkeeper Joan Semple serves homemade treats to guests at breakfast. She prepares jam when fruit is at its peak and always has a variety on hand. Peach jam flecked with bright red cherries is a house specialty.

20 peaches, peeled, pitted and mashed

2 oranges, zest and juice

1 bottle cherries, 4-ounce size, chopped

6 cups sugar

Prepare peaches and place in a large glass bowl. Stir in orange zest, juice and chopped cherries. Add sugar and stir until completely dissolved. Cover with plastic wrap and let stand 8 hours.

Bring fruit to a boil over medium high heat. Reduce heat and simmer, stirring frequently, until mixture thickens.

Bottle in sterilized jars and refrigerate for immediate use or treat with a water bath for extended term storage.

Yields 4 cups.

MURRAY MANOR PEACH BUTTER

The yummy flavour of fresh peaches is present in this simple-to-prepare jam.

20 large ripe peaches, peeled, pitted and coarsely chopped

4 cups sugar

Place peaches and sugar in a large saucepan over medium heat and bring to a boil. Immediately reduce heat and simmer fruit, stirring frequently, until thickened.

Seal in sterilized jars for immediate use and treat with a water bath for longer storage. Yields 4 cups.

NEW BRUNSWICK POACHED PEARS

HOME PORT HISTORIC INN,
SAINT JOHN, NB

Innkeeper Ralph Holyoke lets the weather dictate how he serves this delightful breakfast dish of poached pears! In the cool damp days of autumn he serves them warm, while during the bright cheery mornings of summer, he serves them at room temperature. Whatever the weather or your mood, I'm sure you will enjoy them.

zest of 1 large orange

1/2 cup maple syrup

2 medium to large pears, peeled, halved and cored

chocolate shavings

4 teaspoons butter

fresh mint sprigs, as garnish

In a non-stick frying pan, place orange zest and maple syrup and bring to a strong simmer over medium heat. Place in the pear halves, cut side down, and simmer 3–4 minutes. Turn pears and continue to simmer for 3–4 minutes longer, stirring gently to avoid burning. When pears are tender, remove from pan, reserving the syrup.

To serve, sprinkle chocolate shavings over two serving plates. Place two pear halves, cut side down, over shavings. Quickly return pan to heat and add butter, bring to a boil stirring constantly. Spoon mixture over the pears and garnish with a sprig of mint.

Serves 2.

New Brunswick Poached Pears as served by innkeeper Ralph Holyoke, ▶
at Home Port Historic Inn, Saint John, NB

PEACHES 'N' CREAM CRÊPES

KAULBACK HOUSE HISTORIC INN, LUNENBURG, NS

Depending upon the availability of fresh peaches, these sweet crêpes are a breakfast specialty at Lunenburg's Kaulback House!

8 6-inch crêpes, recipe follows

3 tablespoons light cream cheese, softened

1 1/2 tablespoon sugar

3 tablespoons light sour cream

1 tablespoon puréed peaches

3 large peaches, peeled, pitted and coarsely chopped

Fresh Peach Sauce, recipe follows

Preheat oven to 350°F. In a small bowl, mix together cream cheese, sugar, sour cream and puréed peaches. Divide filling between crêpes, top with coarsely chopped peaches and roll. Place crêpes in an ovenproof dish and bake until hot and bubbly, approximately 20 minutes. To serve, top with warm Fresh Peach Sauce.

Yields 4 servings.

Crêpes (supplied by author)

3/4 cup flour

1/2 teaspoon salt

1 teaspoon baking powder

2 tablespoons powdered sugar (optional)

2 eggs

2/3 cup milk

1 1/3 cup water

1/2 teaspoon vanilla

Sift flour and resift with remaining dry ingredients. In a separate bowl beat eggs, milk, water and vanilla. Make a well in dry ingredients, pour in liquids and combine with a few swift strokes. The batter will be slightly lumpy.

Lightly oil a skillet over moderate heat. Add a small amount of the batter and tip the skillet to spread. When lightly browned, flip crêpe and brown the other side. Yields 14–16 crêpes.

Fresh Peach Sauce

2 peaches, peeled, pitted and chopped

2 teaspoons fresh orange juice

Using a blender, purée fruit. Place fruit and orange juice in a small saucepan and warm over medium heat. Serve warm.

Indulge yourself with Peaches 'n' Cream Crêpes, prepared at ▶ Kaulback House Historic Inn, Lunenburg, NS

APRICOT GLAZED PEARS

KAULBACK HOUSE HISTORIC INN,
LUNENBURG, NS

*Karen Padovani of Kaulback House serves fresh
fruits of the season to her breakfast guests. Her
Apricot Glazed Pears are a delightful combination
of flavours and easy to prepare.*

2 large pears

3 tablespoons apricot jam

2 tablespoons orange juice

ground nutmeg, as garnish

Preheat oven to 350°F. Peel and halve pears,
carefully removing core. Place in an
ovenproof baking dish and set aside.

In a small bowl, mix together the apricot jam
and orange juice. Pour over pear halves and
bake until bubbly, approximately 30 minutes.

Dust with ground nutmeg and serve warm.

Yields 4 servings.

PEACH AND ALMOND JAM

*This jam is made without the addition of pectin. It
is equally delicious as a topping for vanilla ice
cream or a cream filled crêpe.*

6 cups fresh peaches, peeled and
roughly chopped

3 tablespoons fresh lemon juice

4 cups sugar

1 1/2 teaspoon almond extract

Prepare peaches and combine with lemon
juice and sugar in a large saucepan. Bring to
a boil over medium high heat, immediately
reduce heat and simmer until slightly
thickened, approximately 30 minutes.
Remove from burner, skim off foam and
stir in almond extract.

Bottle in sterilized jars and refrigerate for
immediate use or treat in a water bath for
extended storage.

Yields 4-5 cups.

*A creation of the innkeeper, Apricot Glazed Pears as served in the ▶
breakfast room of Kaulback House Historic Inn, Lunenburg, NS*

APPETIZERS, SOUPS AND SALADS

The wonderful thing about salads and soups is that there are no limits on the ingredients. Today's chefs are very adept at how they create tantalizing new ideas from the bounty of the orchards — peaches, pears and plums!

◄ *A warm Brie and Pear Tarte as served at the Dunes Café, Brackley Beach, PEI*

BRIE AND PEAR TARTE

THE DUNES CAFÉ, BRACKLEY BEACH, PEI

Pistou, the French word for Italy's pesto, is prepared by chef Shaun McKay in a blender. Any unused pistou may be bottled, covered with a thin coating of olive oil and refrigerated for several days.

3 tablespoons pistou (recipe follows)

7-inch pizza crust or 7-inch pita bread

1 ripe pear, unpeeled, cored and thinly sliced

2 or 3 ounce round of brie

Preheat oven to 350°F. Spread pistou evenly over crust or pita bread and top with pear slices. Slice brie and place on top of pears. Bake until brie melts and browns slightly, approximately 10–15 minutes.

Pistou

2 cloves of garlic

2 tablespoons cashews

1/8 teaspoon salt

1/4 teaspoon freshly ground black pepper

3/4 cup tightly packed fresh cilantro, coarse stems removed

1/3 cup olive oil

1/2 cup parmesan cheese

Place all ingredients in a food processor and blend until fully chopped.

Yields 3/4 cup.

SMOKED HADDOCK SOUP WITH PEARS AND SEARED SCALLOPS

LES FOUGÈRES RESTAURANT, CHELSEA, PQ

Chefs Jennifer and Charlie Part combine the subtle flavours of smoked haddock, fresh pear and curry in this magnificent soup which is really a meal in a bowl!

8 ounces smoked haddock fillet

1 small onion, chopped

1 small poached pear, chopped

2 tablespoons butter

2 teaspoons curry powder

1 large potato, peeled and chopped

3 cups good quality chicken stock

1 cup pear juice

2 tablespoons heavy cream

2 teaspoons frozen orange juice concentrate, undiluted

salt and pepper, to taste

12 small sea scallops

zest of 1 small orange

fresh cilantro sprigs for garnish

Refresh haddock with several changes of water and break into bite sized chunks, being careful to remove any attached skin. Sauté onion and pear in 1 tablespoon of the butter until onion is translucent. Add curry powder, potato, haddock, stock and pear juice and simmer until potato is soft, approximately 15 minutes. Purée mixture and strain through a fine sieve. Return mixture to a clean pot and add cream and orange juice concentrate. Reheat gently and season with salt and pepper..

To serve, heat remaining butter in a sauté pan and quickly sear scallops on one side only, until caramelized. Divide soup between four bowls, garnish with scallops, orange zest and cilantro sprigs.

Serves 4.

SPINACH SALAD CHERISHED WITH PEPPERED STRAWBERRY VINAIGRETTE

LIBERTINE CAFÉ AND KITCHEN, HALIFAX, NS

In this innovative salad, Chef Peter Woodworth enhances the flavours of fresh fruit with a delightful vinaigrette. The decision to peel the plum and pear depends upon personal taste. If the fruits are fully ripe the peel provides a subtle texture to the salad.

12 ounces fresh spinach

1 peach, peeled

1 plum

1 pear

1 tablespoon lemon juice

Peppered Strawberry and Feta Vinaigrette, recipe follows

crumbled feta cheese, as garnish

Pick large stems from spinach then wash and spin dry. Break into bite-sized pieces and place in a large salad bowl.

Slice the peach, plum and pear into chunks and toss lightly with lemon juice in a small bowl.

Scatter fruit on top of spinach.

Divide salad between four serving plates and drizzle with Peppered Strawberry and Feta Vinaigrette. Garnish with additional feta cheese, if desired.

Peppered Strawberry and Feta Vinaigrette

1/2 cup fresh or frozen strawberries

1 teaspoon freshly ground black pepper

1/8 cup feta cheese

1 tablespoon liquid honey

3 tablespoons red wine vinegar

1/4 cup olive oil

Put all ingredients except olive oil into food processor and process on high until mixture is smooth. With motor running on medium, slowly add olive oil. Blend until creamy but not too thick.

Yields 1 cup.

Spinach Salad with Peppered Strawberry Vinaigrette, the creation of chef Peter Woodworth, ▶
Libertine Café and Kitchen, Halifax, NS

PEACH AND SQUASH SOUP

BLOMIDON INN, WOLFVILLE, NS

Innkeepers are quick to learn that what is fresh, is best. Chef Sean Laceby at the Blomidon Inn prepares this delightful soup with squash grown in the inn's extensive gardens and uses fresh fruit from a local market. He adds the heavy cream as a decorative touch!

2 tablespoons butter

1/2 cup chopped celery

1 small onion, chopped

2 3/4 cups squash, peeled diced

2 cups fresh or canned peach slices

2 1/2 cups chicken stock

2 - 3 tablespoons liquid honey

3/4 teaspoon ground nutmeg

salt and pepper, to taste

3/4 cup heavy cream (35% m.f.)

Melt butter in a large saucepan over low heat and add celery and onion. Sauté approximately 5 minutes. Add squash, peach slices and stock and bring to a boil. Reduce heat and simmer until squash is tender. Stir in honey, nutmeg and season with salt and pepper. Cool slightly, then purée in batches in a blender. Add cream and return to serving temperature, being careful not to boil.

Serves 6–8.

RADICCHIO & ENDIVE SALAD WITH MAPLE & PEACH DRESSING

THE BRIARS RESORT, JACKSON'S POINT, ONT.

Chef Trevor Ledlie of the Briars Resort uses a medley of greens in this decorative salad.

2 Belgium endive

2 butterhead lettuces

1 radicchio

1 pear, sliced into match stick-sized slices

Maple Peach Dressing, recipe follows

Arrange the endive and butterhead around the outside of your plates. Slice radicchio and place in the centre, drizzle with Maple Peach Dressing and sprinkle with pear slices. Serves 6 - 8.

Maple Peach Dressing

1/2 cup white wine vinegar

2 medium peaches, peeled and pitted

1/4 teaspoon jalapeno pepper, chopped

2 tablespoons maple syrup

1/4 teaspoon chopped parsley

juice of 1/2 lime

1 1/2 cups olive oil

Combine vinegar, peaches, jalapeno, syrup, parsley and lime in food processor or blender and combine. With mixer running add oil in a slow stream, until emulsified. Yields 2 cups.

Swirled with cream, Peach and Squash Soup from Wolfville's Blomidon Inn is an ▶ artistic masterpiece

FALL HARVEST PEAR CHUTNEY

TATTINGSTONE INN,
WOLFVILLE, NS

*Several fruit trees grace the beautiful grounds of
the Tattingstone Inn and Betsey Harwood uses her
pears to make this spicy chutney. She advises that
this recipe may be adjusted to make peach, apple or
even cranberry chutney.*

8 cups peeled and cubed pears

4-5 cloves garlic, minced

1 small onion, diced

1 cup raisins or dried currants

3 cups packed brown sugar

1 1/2 teaspoon ground ginger

1 teaspoon dried mustard

1 1/2 teaspoon cinnamon

1 teaspoon crushed chili peppers

1/3 teaspoon salt

1 cup cider vinegar

Combine all ingredients in a large stainless
steel kettle, bring slowly to a boil. Cook,
uncovered and stirring occasionally, reducing
heat as chutney begins to thicken,
approximately 1 1/4 hour.

Bottle in sterilized jars for immediate use or
process in a water bath for longer storage.

Yields 6 cups.

PEAR AND BLUE CHEESE BAGUETTE

CHARLOTTE LANE CAFÉ AND
CRAFTS, SHELBURNE, NS

*Chef Roland Glauser changes his menu with the
seasons. This late summer appetizer depicts the
very best of his innovative cuisine.*

1 1/2 ounces blue cheese, crumbled

2 tablespoons egg-based mayonnaise

salt and pepper, to taste

6-8 slices fresh Baguette

1 pear, peeled, cored and poached

Slightly warm cheese and mix with
mayonnaise. Season with salt and pepper
and refrigerate.

Preheat broiler. Slice pear into 6–8 equal
slices. Slice baguette and place on a baking
sheet. Spread with cheese mixture, top with a
pear slice and broil until well heated and crisp.
Yields 6–8 slices.

*Chef Roland Glauser of the Charlotte Lane Café and Crafts Restaurant serves his Pear and ▶
Blue Cheese Baguette during the height of the pear season.*

KELTIC'S CHILLED PEACH SOUP

KELTIC LODGE, INGONISH
BEACH, NS

The chef at Keltic Lodge suggests you garnish this beautiful soup with large strawberries. If fresh strawberries are not in season, try kiwi slices or other fruits.

8 fresh peaches

1/4 cup extra fine white sugar

1 cup sweet white wine

2 cups water

pinch of cinnamon

1 cup white wine (second amount)

8 large strawberries, sliced for garnish

Make a cross on the top of each peach and drop into boiling water for 30 seconds and then in cold water until the skin peels back. Remove the pit and chop the flesh.

In a medium pot combine sugar, sweet white wine, water, cinnamon and peaches. Simmer on low until peaches are soft. Pour into a blender and purée.

Press mixture through a coarse strainer. Add the second amount of white wine and chill overnight.

Serve with sliced strawberries as a garnish.

Yields 6–8 servings.

CRAZY BEAN SALAD

CHARLOTTE LANE CAFÉ & CRAFTS,
SHELBURNE, NS

Chef Roland Glauser of the Charlotte Lane is an innovative cook! His combination of fresh green beans, pears and pineapple is showy, as well as being a delightful combination of flavours.

2 pounds fresh green beans, ends removed

2–3 pears, cored and diced in 1-inch cubes

1/2 fresh pineapple, diced in 1-inch cubes

Crazy Bean Salad Dressing, recipe follows

1/2 cup toasted almond slivers

assorted salad greens to serve 6

Prepare and cook green beans until al dente, and immediately cool off in ice water. Drain and set aside. Dice pear and pineapple. Combine fruit and vegetables with enough dressing to cover, allowing to marinate in the refrigerator for a few minutes. Serve salad over a bed of assorted greens, sprinkled with toasted almond slivers. Serves 6.

Crazy Bean Salad Dressing

1/2 cup sour cream

1 1/4 cups egg-based mayonnaise

6 tablespoons fresh tarragon, chopped

1/4 cup red wine vinegar

In a small bowl whisk together all ingredients and refrigerate. Yields 2 cup dressing.

Layers of nutritious fruits and vegetables make up Crazy Bean Salad from ▶
Charlotte Lane Café and Crafts, Shelburne, NS

FENNEL SALAD WITH CARAMELIZED PEARS

ARBOR VIEW INN, LUNENBURG, NS

Owner-chef Daniel Orovec marries the subtle flavours of fennel and pears in this attractive salad. Making his salad cups out of radicchio leaves, he reserves the smaller inner leaves for future use.

1 large fennel bulb

Arbor View Vinaigrette, recipe follows

1 cup sugar

1/2 cup water

2 pears, peeled, cored and quartered

radicchio lettuce leaves

fresh cilantro sprigs or chive shoots, as garnish

Remove outer layer of fennel and quarter. Thinly slice fennel using a sharp knife, or mandolin, and marinate in Arbor View Vinaigrette for at least 1 hour.

Combine sugar and water in a small saucepan over medium high heat. Boil, watching closely, until syrup is a honey caramel colour. Add pears, reduce heat and simmer until pears are tender. Drain and set aside.

To serve, break off 4 radicchio leaves to form 4 "cups". Centre one on each of 4 salad plates. With a slotted spoon, remove fennel from marinade and reserve vinaigrette.

Divide fennel between the 4 cups, allowing a little to spill out on to the plate. Arrange the pears on the plate and drizzle a little reserved vinaigrette over salad.

Garnish with fresh herbs.

Yields 4 servings.

Arbor View Vinaigrette

1/4 cup sherry vinegar

2 teaspoons Dijon mustard

1 shallot, finely minced

salt and pepper, to taste

1/3 cup walnut oil

1/3 cup olive oil

In a blender or food processor combine vinegar, mustard and shallot. With machine running, add oils in a fine stream, processing until emulsified. Season with salt and pepper.

When is a salad a work of art? When it is Fennel Salad with Caramelized Pears ▶ served at Lunenburg's Arbor Inn

ACCOMPANIMENTS AND MAIN ENTRÉES

*I*n the interest of making use of in-season fruit, the chefs have developed wonderful recipes incorporating peaches, pears and plums. From spicy chutneys and relishes to seafood with fruit salsa, they have found that these flavourful fruits enhance many kinds of entrées.

◄ *Cape Sante con Pesche is the delicious creation of James MacDougall at La Perla, Dartmouth, NS*

CAPE SANTE CON PESCHE

LA PERLA DINING ROOM,
DARTMOUTH, NS

Chef James MacDougall serves this colourful scallop dish with a rice or orzo pilaf. He dredges the scallops with very finely ground corn meal.

1 1/4 pound sea scallops

1/2 cup corn flour

4 tablespoons butter

2 large peaches, peeled, pitted and sliced

2 tablespoons brown sugar

1/2 cup Southern Comfort liqueur

1/2 medium-sized red bell pepper, in julienne strips

salt and pepper, to taste

Dredge scallops in corn flour, shaking off excess and set aside.

In a large skillet melt butter over high heat. Add scallops to pan and cook until scallops are half done, approximately 2 minutes. Add sliced peaches and sugar. Stir in Southern Comfort and simmer to glaze scallops and peaches. Toss in red pepper strips and season with salt and pepper.

Yields 4 servings.

BLUE PLUM CHUTNEY

MURRAY MANOR BED & BREAKFAST,
YARMOUTH, NS

Innkeeper Joan Semple prepares this delightful chutney when plums are at the peak of their season. It is a wonderful accompaniment to chicken and pork dishes.

3 pounds blue plums, pitted and finely chopped

1 pound apples, cored and chopped

1 pound onions, finely chopped

1/2 pound pitted dates, chopped

1/2 pound sultana raisins

4 cups sugar

2 1/2 cups malt vinegar

3 tablespoons pickling spice

2 tablespoons fresh ginger, finely chopped

Combine plums, apples, onions, dates and raisins in a large saucepan. Add sugar and vinegar, stirring until sugar is dissolved.

Place pickling spice and ginger in a spice bag and add to mixture. Bring to a boil, reduce heat and simmer 1 1/2 to 2 hours.

Remove spice bag and bottle the chutney in sterilized jars for immediate use, or treat with a water bath for long-term storage.

Yields 6–8 cups.

CHRISTMAS CHUTNEY

JUBILEE COTTAGE COUNTRY INN, WALLACE, NS

*Daphne Dominy tells me that the wonderful combination of
fruit and spices is marvellous with turkey.*

3 quarts ripe tomatoes, skinned, seeded and diced

4 large onions, chopped

2 stalks celery, chopped

1 green pepper, seeded and chopped

1/4 cup pickling salt

4 pears, peeled and diced

4 peaches, peeled and diced

4 apples, peeled and diced

1 1/2 cups vinegar

1 1/2 tablespoons pickling spice, tied in a cheesecloth bag

3/4 teaspoon celery seed

1/8 teaspoon cayenne pepper

4 cups brown sugar

Combine tomatoes, onions, celery and green pepper in a large glass bowl and sprinkle with salt. Cover and let stand in a cool place overnight.

To prepare chutney, drain vegetables and place in a large stock pot. Add pears, peaches, vinegar, pickling spice, celery seed and cayenne. Bring to a boil, reduce heat and simmer 1 hour, stirring occasionally. Add sugar and simmer an additional 30 minutes, stirring constantly so the mixture does not stick to the bottom of the pot.

Remove cheesecloth bag and pour chutney into sterilized jars and seal for immediate use or treat in a water bath for longer storage.

Yields 8–10 cups.

DUNDEE MAPLE ROASTED PORK TENDERLOIN WITH FRUIT

THE DUNDEE ARMS HOTEL, CHARLOTTETOWN, PEI

Chef Austin Clement advises that this is an excellent dish for entertaining because the confiture of fruit may be prepared while you roast the pork. At the inn they serve this dish with roast potatoes and grilled vegetables.

2 pork tenderloins, 3/4 pounds each

1/4 cup pure maple syrup, divided

1/3 cup Pomery mustard, divided

1 teaspoon salt, divided

1 tablespoon whole peppers, cracked, divided

3 1/2 tablespoons clarified butter

1/3 cup fresh peaches, peeled and cut in large dice

1/3 cup fresh plums, cut in large dice

1/3 cup fresh pears, cut in large dice

3 tablespoons brown sugar

1 tablespoon cumin seed

1/4 cup white vinegar

Preheat oven to 350°F.

Trim pork tenderloins of all fat and silverskin.

In a small bowl mix together half of the maple syrup, mustard, salt and cracked pepper to make a marinade. Brush on pork until completely covered, pouring any excess over meat. Roast until meat thermometer reads 150–160°F, approximately 20 minutes.

While pork is roasting prepare fruit confiture. Sauté fruit in clarified butter over medium heat approximately 5 minutes, stirring frequently. Add remaining mustard, salt and pepper, brown sugar, cumin seed and vinegar. Continue cooking another 2–3 minutes, then add remaining maple syrup and cook an additional three minutes.

To serve, spoon a small amount of fruit mixture on four plates. Slice pork into medallions and arrange on sauce. Drizzle pork with remaining fruit.

Serves 4.

Dundee Arm's Maple Roasted Pork Tenderloin is served with a delightful ▶ Cranberry Fruit Compote

GRILLED SALMON WITH PLUM SALSA

LA PERLA DINING ROOM, DARTMOUTH, NS

This is a simple but delightfully "fresh" dish. The salsa must be prepared early in the day in order for the flavours to blend. At La Perla, chef James MacDougall suggest serving the salmon with a crisp salad and a white Zinfindel!

1/4 cup dried cranberries

2 tablespoons white wine

3 large Santa Rossa plums, pitted and diced

1/2 Bosc pear, diced

2 green onions, diced

1/2 medium red onion, diced

1/2 yellow pepper, diced

3 ounces fresh pineapple, diced

2 tablespoons honey

1 tablespoon fresh ginger, minced

4 salmon fillets, boneless and skinless, 6 ounces each

flour for dusting

salt and pepper, to taste

1 tablespoon olive oil

In a small bowl soak cranberries in wine to plump. Cut all vegetables and fruits into a uniform medium dice. Place all fruit and vegetables in a bowl, stir in cranberries, honey and ginger. Let stand 2 to 3 hours so flavours will blend.

Preheat oven to 375° F.

Rinse and pat dry salmon fillets. Lightly dust with flour, season with salt and pepper. Heat oil over high heat in a heavy oven-proof skillet. Add fillets and sear, turning once. Place skillet in oven and bake 4–5 minutes, until done.

To serve, place a generous spoonful of salsa on plate and top with salmon fillet.

Serves 4.

Tart Plum Salsa is an ideal accompaniment to La Perla's Grilled Salmon ▶

ROAST LOIN OF LAMB WITH GRILLED PEARS AND CINNAMON SAUCE

INN AT BAY FORTUNE, BAY FORTUNE, PEI

Chef Michael Smith serves his lamb on a bed of mint barley in the full presentation as shown in the photo. For more of his creations, watch Life channel where he hosts a weekly program called "Inn Chef"!

1 boneless loin of lamb, 1 1/2–2 pounds

2 garlic cloves

salt and pepper, to taste

2 tablespoons butter

Cinnamon Sauce, recipe follows

Grilled Pears, recipe follows

fresh mint sprigs, as garnish

Preheat oven to 325°F.

Mince the garlic and rub it directly on the lamb. Season with salt and pepper.

Melt butter over medium heat in a non-stick ovenproof pan. Sear roast, turning to ensure that it is evenly coloured. Remove to oven and finish off until roast reaches desired internal temperature on a meat thermometer (145°F rare, 155°F medium), approximately 15–18 minutes per pound. Remove from oven, tent with foil and let stand 10 minutes before serving.

To serve, reheat sauce and grill pears. Pour 3–4 tablespoons of sauce onto a large, hot, dinner plate and add the sliced lamb and pears. Garnish with mint sprigs. Serves 4.

Cinnamon Sauce

1 cup chopped onion

2 tablespoons butter

3 garlic cloves, minced

1 1/2 cups lamb or chicken broth

1 teaspoon ground cinnamon

salt and pepper, to taste

In a heavy frying pan brown onions in butter until they are golden brown and reduced in volume. Add garlic and continue cooking an additional 2 minutes. Stir in broth and bring to a boil, reduce heat and simmer 20 minutes. Season with cinnamon, salt and pepper and process in a blender until smooth. Keep warm.

Grilled Pears

3 tablespoons extra virgin olive oil

1 tablespoon Dijon mustard

1 tablespoon red wine vinegar

salt and pepper

2 ripe Bartlett or D'Anjou pears

Whisk together the oil, mustard, vinegar, salt and pepper. Cut the pears into thick slices, dip into oil mixture and let rest 1 hour. Grill the pears just before serving time, turning evenly.

Roast Loin of Lamb as prepared by the innovative Michael Smith of Inn at Bay Fortune ▶

DESSERTS

*O*h, dessert lovers, wait no longer! Here are the most mouth-watering delights that bring out the best in peaches, plums and pears.

◄ *A large dessert, Whitman Inn's Rustic Three-Plum Tart is ideal for a crowd*

RUSTIC THREE-PLUM TART

WHITMAN INN, KEMPT, NS

This is a large tart, ideal for entertaining. Innkeeper Nancy Gurnham suggests that you allow the crust to look a bit "ragged," thus living up to its name "Rustic Three Plum Tart." At the inn, they slice this large tart using a pizza cutter!

1/2 cup sugar

1/3 cup pecans or walnuts

1/4 cup flour

1/2 teaspoon cinnamon

1/4 teaspoon nutmeg

pinch allspice

1 1/2 – 2 pounds yellow, red and purple plums

2 cups flour (2nd amount)

4 tablespoons sugar

1/2 teaspoon salt

2/3 cup cold butter, in cubes

1 teaspoon lemon juice

cold water

1 egg yolk

2 tablespoons milk

1 1/2 teaspoons sugar

1/2 cup heavy cream, (35% m.f.) whipped, as garnish

Using a food processor combine sugar, nuts, flour, cinnamon, nutmeg and allspice until finely ground. Set aside.

Wash, dry and pit plums. Do not peel, but slice or quarter into uniform size. Set aside.

In a large bowl combine flour, sugar and salt. Using a pastry blender cut in butter cubes until mixture resembles a coarse meal. In a small bowl combine lemon juice plus enough cold water to measure 1/2 cup, whisk in egg yolk. Quickly incorporate liquids with flour mixture stirring only until well blended and dough holds together. Gather dough into a ball shape, flatten slightly and wrap in plastic wrap. Refrigerate 15 minutes.

Preheat oven to 425°F.

Roll out dough into a 14–15 inch circle on a floured surface. Transfer to pizza pan and spread the ground nut mixture over the of the pastry leaving 2–3 inches margin around the edge. Place plums over nut mixture. Gently fold the uncovered pastry up and over to the outside edge of the fruit. Brush crust with milk and sprinkle with sugar. Bake 12–15 minutes, reduce temperature to 375°F. and continue baking until pastry's golden and fruit is bubbly. Cool.

Serve in wedges garnished with whipped cream.

PEAR AND HAZELNUT FLAN

HOTEL NEWFOUNDLAND, ST. JOHN'S, NFLD

Hotel Newfoundland's pastry chef, Steve Shepherd, serves these delicacies with a scoop of Cream Cheese Granite on pool of Strawberry Coulis.

12 ounces frozen puff pastry, thawed in refrigerator

Frangipane, recipe follows

1 pound pears, peeled, cored and thinly sliced

1/3 cup butter, melted

1/2 teaspoon vanilla

1 egg, whisked with 1 1/2 teaspoons water

Cream Cheese Granite, recipe follows

On a lightly floured surface, roll out puff pastry to a 1/4-inch thickness. Cut into 4 squares, 5x 5-inch. Divide the frangipane between the pastry squares, spreading close to the edges. Spread sliced pears evenly over frangipane.

In a small bowl combine melted butter and vanilla and brush fruit. Brush exposed edges of pastry with egg wash and fold, corner to corner, forming a triangle. Refrigerate pastries for 20 minutes.

Preheat oven to 375°F. Brush pastries with remaining egg wash and bake until puffed and browned, approximately 15 minutes. Serve with a small scoop of Cream Cheese Granite.

Frangipane

1/3 cup butter, softened

1/3 cup sugar

1 egg

2 teaspoons freshly squeezed lemon juice

1/4 cup flour

1/2 cup roasted hazelnuts, ground

With an electric mixer combine butter and sugar until light and fluffy. Add egg and lemon juice, beating until well blended. Stir in flour and ground hazelnuts, mixing until blended.

Cream Cheese Granite

4 ounces cream cheese, softened

1/4 cup sugar

1/4 cup water

juice of 1 lemon

Place cream cheese in a blender and process until very soft.

Combine sugar and water in a small saucepan and bring to a boil, cooking 5 minutes to produce a simple syrup. Remove from heat and let cool 10–15 minutes.

With blender running, slowly add syrup and lemon juice to cream cheese. Process until well blended, then refrigerate mixture until solidified, at least 2 hours.

AMARETTI PEACHES

SHADOW LAWN COUNTRY INN, ROTHESAY, NB

Chef Patricia Bullock advises that while fresh peaches are preferred, preserved peach halves may be used. In this instance, omit the lemon juice and reduce the baking time to 15–20 minutes. She serves the peaches with a generous scoop of ice cream. Amaretti cookies are crisp almond flavoured macaroons and are available at Italian-style markets.

4 ripe peaches

juice of 1 lemon

1 cup crushed amaretti cookies

1/4 cup marsala wine or peach brandy

1/4 cup butter, softened

1/2 teaspoon vanilla extract

1/4 cup sugar

1 egg yolk

Preheat oven to 350°F.

Peel peaches and cut in half. Remove stone and hollow out the centre by scooping out a little of the flesh with a melon baller. Brush the peach halves with lemon juice to prevent them from discolouring.

Combine the crushed amaretti cookies with the wine and allow to sit for a few minutes to soften crumbs. Add the remaining ingredients and mix well.

Place the peach halves in a shallow baking dish and fill with the amaretti mixture. Bake until the fruit is soft and the topping slightly browned, approximately 30 – 40 minutes.

Serve warm or cool, garnished with whipped cream. Yields 4 servings.

*Almond infused Amaretti Peaches are the creation of chef Patricia Bullock of ▶
Shadow Lawn Inn, Rothesay, NB*

PEACH AND CHOCOLATE PARFAIT

CATHERINE MCKINNON'S SPOT O' TEA RESTAURANT, STANLEY BRIDGE, PEI

While this restaurant is famous for its Maritime fish cakes and homemade beans, nobody, but nobody, leaves without sampling pastry chef Whitney Armstrong's delectable desserts.

4 ounces semi-sweet dark chocolate

2 peaches, peeled, pitted and puréed

4 tablespoons peach schnapps

2 cups heavy cream (35% m.f.) whipped

1 whole egg and 5 egg yolks

1/2 cup sugar

Orange Peach Sauce, recipe follows

16 Coconut Brandy Snaps, recipe follows

fresh mint, as garnish

Melt chocolate in the top half of a double boiler over simmering water. Set aside. Purée peaches and set aside. Whip cream to a soft peak consistency and refrigerate.

Over medium heat whisk egg yolks with sugar. Using a candy thermometer, cook mixture to a soft ball stage, 240°F. Remove from heat and whip with an electric mixer until volume doubles. Set aside to cool.

Using a spatula, fold whipped cream into egg mixture. Divide mixture, folding the melted chocolate into the first bowl, and the peach purée into the second. Using 8 decorative molds, pour chocolate mixture into 4 molds, and peach mixture into the remaining 4 molds. Freeze.

To serve, drizzle plates with Orange Peach Sauce. Position a Coconut Brandy Snap on the sauce, unmold a chocolate parfait on the cookie, top with another cookie , and the peach parfait. Garnish with mint. Serves 4.

Orange Peach Sauce

1 cup orange juice

4 tablespoons peach schnapps

1 tablespoon each cornstarch and sugar

Bring all ingredients to a boil over medium heat, stirring constantly. When mixture begins to thicken, remove from heat and cool.

Coconut Brandy Snaps

1/2 cup butter, softened

1/2 cup icing sugar

4 tablespoons shredded coconut

1/3 cup corn syrup

1 cup flour

1/2 teaspoon brandy

Preheat oven to 325°F. Combine butter, icing sugar, coconut and corn syrup in a saucepan and bring to a boil over medium heat. Remove from burner and stir in flour and brandy. Cool. Line 2 baking sheets with parchment paper and drop 1/2 tablespoon of cookie dough on sheet allowing 8 inches between snaps. Gently spread dough into even rounds. Bake until browned, approximately 10–12 minutes. Let stand 1 minute, then remove to a wire rack to cool.

*Peach and Chocolate Parfaits, a chocolate lovers delight as prepared by chef Whitney ▶
Armstrong of Catherine McKinnon's Spot O'Tea Restaurant, Stanley Bridge, PEI*

WHITE WINE AND PEAR SORBET

THE JUBILEE COTTAGE COUNTRY INN, WALLACE, NS

Daphne Dominy serves this sorbet as a light dessert or as a refresher between the salad and main course. She finds that Jost Riesling from a neighbouring winery is just perfect for the recipe!

8 large pears, peeled, cored and chopped

1 cup white sugar

1 cup filtered water

2 tablespoons lemon juice

1 cup medium dry white wine

Combine pears, sugar, water and lemon juice in a saucepan and bring to a boil over high heat. Reduce heat and simmer, covered for 15 minutes or until pears are very soft. Remove from burner and strain, reserving poaching liquid.

Place pears in a blender in batches and process until very smooth. Add pears to poaching liquid and cool. Stir in wine and chill. Process the mixture in an electric ice-cream maker following the manufacturer's instructions.

Yields 3 cups.

ANGEL PEACH PIE

THE NORMAWAY INN, MARGAREE VALLEY, NS

The Normaway Inn, tucked into a Cape Breton valley, offers hospitality and great dining in the old Scottish tradition. Innkeeper David MacDonald shared this recipe some years ago.

1 1/2 cups graham cracker crumbs

1/3 cup melted butter

5 egg whites

1/4 teaspoon salt

1/2 teaspoon cream of tartar

4 peaches, peeled, pitted and sliced

1 1/2 cups heavy cream (35% m.f.)

3/4 cup coconut, toasted

Preheat oven to 275° F.

Combine graham crumbs and butter and press into a 9-inch pie plate.

Prepare meringue by beating egg whites, salt and cream of tartar until stiff peaks form. Pour into crust, spreading evenly to the sides and bake for 1 1/4 hours. Cool.

Arrange well drained peach slices on top of cooled meringue.

Whip cream until soft peaks form. Sprinkle with sugar and continue beating until cream is stiff. Spread cream over peaches and sprinkle with toasted coconut.

Serves 6–8.

Smooth as silk, Jubilee Cottages and Country Inn's White Wine and Pear Sorbet is a delight. ▶

BREAD PUDDING WITH PEACHES AND WARM RUM SAUCE

THE DUNES CAFÉ, BRACKLEY BEACH, PEI

Bread pudding with a difference! At the Dunes, Chef Shaun McKay serves his pudding laced with peaches and a delicious Warm Rum Sauce.

5 cups day-old bread, cut into cubes

14-ounce can sliced peaches

3 large eggs

1/2 cup sugar

1 1/2 teaspoon cinnamon

2 cups liquid (reserved peach juice + milk)

Rum Sauce, recipe follows

Preheat oven to 325°F.

Place bread cubes in a large bowl.

Drain peach slices, reserving liquid, and add peaches to the bowl.

In a separate bowl, beat together eggs, sugar, cinnamon and 2 cups liquid. Combine with bread and pour into a greased 2-quart baking dish. Let stand until bread absorbs moisture.

Place the dish in a slightly larger pan and add hot water to come halfway up the sides of the baking dish. Bake until custard is set and dessert is a light golden brown, approximately 1 hour.

Serve warm with Rum Sauce.

Serves 6–8.

Rum Sauce

1/4 cup butter

1 cup brown sugar

1/2 teaspoon vanilla

1/4 cup dark rum

1/4 teaspoon cinnamon

1 cup water

1 tablespoon cornstarch, dissolved in 1 1/2 tablespoons cold water

Bring all ingredients to a boil, reduce heat and simmer, stirring constantly until slightly thickened. Serve warm.

Bread pudding has been elevated to gourmet fare as the chef of the Dunes Café presents ▶ Bread Pudding with Peaches and Warm Rum Sauce.

PEAR TATIN

CATHERINE MCKINNON'S SPOT O' TEA RESTAURANT, STANLEY BRIDGE, PEI

Pastry Chef Whitney Armstrong serves Pear Tatin warm from the oven, garnished with whipped cream and a scoop of best quality vanilla ice cream. He advises a quick, careful flip in transferring the pie from the pan to the serving plate.

1/2 cup butter

1/4 cup sugar

1 small egg

1 1/2 cups flour

1 cup sugar

1/4 cup water

2 tablespoons butter

4 pears, peeled, cored and sliced

1/2 cup heavy cream (35% m.f.) whipped, as garnish

vanilla ice cream, optional

With an electric mixer on low speed, combine butter and sugar until light and fluffy. Mix in egg, then slowly blend in flour. Wrap dough in plastic wrap and refrigerate 30 minutes.

In a saucepan over medium high heat combine sugar and water. Bring to a hard boil and cook, without stirring, just until mixture is golden brown. Remove from burner and carefully stir in butter. Pour over the bottom of a 10-inch pie plate.

Arrange sliced pears over caramel in the pie plate.

Preheat oven to 375°F. On a lightly floured surface, roll dough to an 10-inch circle. Place dough circle over pears, gently tucking in edges. Bake until the dough is crisp and golden, approximately 45 minutes. Remove from oven and let stand 15 minutes.

To serve, place a large rimmed serving plate upside down on top of the pie, then carefully flip the pan and plate.

Serve warm, garnished with whipped cream or vanilla ice cream. Serves 6–8.

*Caramel-coloured Pear Tatin, presented by the chef of Catherine McKinnon's ▶
Spot O'Tea Restaurant, Stanley Bridge, PEI*

WICKWIRE HOUSE PEACH CARDAMOM CAKE

WICKWIRE HOUSE, KENTVILLE, NS

This is a wonderfully moist cake flavoured with cardamom, an aromatic spice of the ginger family. Serve it with coffee in the morning, in the afternoon with a pot of tea, or simply enjoy as dessert.

1/4 cup brown sugar

1 tablespoon cinnamon

1/2 cup pecans

3 or 4 peaches, peeled, pitted and thinly sliced

1 cup butter, softened

1 cup brown sugar, 2nd amount

2 eggs

1 teaspoon vanilla

2 cups flour

1 teaspoon baking powder

1 1/4 teaspoons baking soda

3/4 teaspoon ground cardamom

1/4 teaspoon salt

1 cup sour cream

icing sugar, for dusting

Preheat oven to 350°F.

In a small bowl combine brown sugar, cinnamon and pecans and set aside. Prepare peaches and set aside in a separate bowl.

With an electric mixer cream butter and 2nd amount of brown sugar until light and fluffy. Add eggs and vanilla and beat well.

In a separate bowl sift together the flour, baking powder, baking soda, cardamon and salt. Fold flour mixture into butter mixture alternately with sour cream, beginning and ending with flour and being careful not to over mix.

Grease and flour a large bundt pan. Spoon 1/3 of the batter into the pan, add 1/2 the nut mixture and 1/2 the peach slices. Add another 1/3 of the batter, then the remaining nuts and peaches. Top with remaining batter and bake 1 1/2 hours until brown on top and a toothpick inserted in the centre comes out clean.

Remove from oven and let stand 10 minutes before turning out on a serving plate. When cool dust with icing sugar.

House delight in innkeeper Darlene Peerless's ▶
Peach Cardamon Cake, from Wickwire House, Kentville, NS

PEACH AND PLUM PHYLLO CHEESECAKE

LA MAISON DINING ROOM, HALIFAX, NS

Chef Karl-Heinz Szielasko uses phyllo pastry as the base for his fruit-filled cheesecake. Paper thin phyllo is fragile and must be kept covered to avoid drying out. The pastry is found in the frozen food section of supermarkets.

1 pound package frozen phyllo pastry

1/3 cup butter, melted

1/4 cup flour

1/2 teaspoon ground almonds

1/3 cup icing sugar

10 ounces cream cheese, at room temperature

3 eggs, lightly beaten

1 teaspoon grated orange zest

1 tablespoon Frangelico liqueur

1/2 peach, peeled, pitted and in small dice

1 plum, peeled, pitted and in small dice

2 tablespoons pistachio nuts, chopped

Thaw phyllo in refrigerator overnight. Carefully remove from package and unfold. Cover immediately with a clean, slightly damp tea towel. Place 1 sheet of phyllo on a work surface, keeping remaining pastry sheets covered. Using a pastry brush, lightly brush with melted butter and cut into 6 to 8 squares 5 x 5 inches. Arrange squares in a 3-inch muffin tin. Repeat this process until you have 4 layers of pastry, arranging each square on a slight angle in the pan, thus creating a flower petal effect.

Preheat oven to 300°F.

In a small bowl, blend together the flour, almonds and sugar; set aside.

In another bowl, using an electric mixer, beat cream cheese until light and fluffy. Add eggs, one at a time, beating until completely combined. Blend in flour mixture, orange zest and Frangelico. Spoon into prepared pastry cups and gently drop in peach and plum pieces. Bake until the centre of the cheesecake is slightly firm and pastry is golden brown, approximately 25 minutes. Cool in pan before removing, then garnish with pistachio nuts.

Serves 6–8.

*Individual little desserts, Peach and Plum Phyllo Cheesecakes ▶
from La Maison, Halifax, NS*

WHITMAN INN PEAR TART

THE WHITMAN INN

At the Whitman Inn, innkeeper Nancy Gurnham is always looking for ways to change her menu. Occasionally she serves the tart on a bed of raspberry coulis, and suggests that apples, peaches or even bananas could replace the pears in this recipe.

1/2 cup butter

1/3 cup sugar

1 cup flour

1/4 teaspoon vanilla

8 ounces cream cheese, softened

1/2 teaspoon vanilla (second amount)

1/2 cup sugar (second amount)

1 egg

4 pears, peeled, cored and sliced

1 egg, beaten

1/3 cup sugar

1/2 teaspoon cinnamon

1/8 teaspoon ground cardamom

1/3 cup chopped walnuts, optional

Preheat oven to 425°F.

Using a food processor combine butter, sugar, flour and vanilla until crumbs begin to hold together. Press crumb mixture over the bottom and 1/2-inch up the sides of a greased 9-inch spring form pan.

Using an electric mixter, combine cheese, 2nd amounts of vanilla and sugar, and egg until smooth. Spread this filling over crust.

Prepare pears and set aside. In a small bowl combine egg, sugar, cinnamon and cardamom. Toss with pears to coat and arrange pears over cheese filling.

Place pan on a cookie sheet and bake in preheated oven for 10 minutes. Reduce temperature to 400°F, sprinkle with nuts if desired and continue to bake until golden brown, approximately 25 minutes.

Slice in wedges and serve either chilled or at room temperature. Serves 8.

Innkeeper Nancy Gurnham of Whitman Inn treats her guests royally with ▶ offerings such as Whitman Inn Pear Tart

ZINFANDEL AFFOGO PERE

LA PERLA DINING ROOM,
DARTMOUTH, NS

Chef James MacDougall prefers to use Bosc pears for this spectacular dessert which should be prepared early in the day and assembled at serving time.

4 large pears, peeled with stems attached

3 cups red wine (Zinfandel)

3/4 cup superfine sugar

1 cinnamon stick

2 egg yolks

2 tablespoons superfine sugar (2nd amount)

1 1/2 ounce Raspberry liqueur

4 ounces Mascarpone cheese

1 cup heavy cream (35% m.f.) whipped

Carefully remove core from bottom of pears with a melon baller.

Place wine in a medium sized saucepan, whisk in 3/4 cup sugar. Add cinnamon stick and pears. Cover pot, bring to a boil then reduce heat to a slow simmer and cook until pears are tender, 20-25 minutes. Remove pears, and continue to reduce wine to syrup consistency. Discard cinnamon stick and cool.

Place a heat proof bowl over a pot of simmering water. Whisk together yolks, sugar and liqueur until thick. Remove from heat and cool. Whisk in Mascarpone cheese until blended, fold in whipped cream and refrigerate.Serve with a dollop of cream mixture on a plate, top with a pear and drizzle with a little chilled wine syrup.

PLUMS MACERATED IN BRANDY

WICKWIRE HOUSE, KENTVILLE, NS

"This is not an instant dessert," cautions innkeeper Darlene Peerless, who bottles her plums in early October for use over the Christmas holidays. Mrs. Peerless adds that they are delicious served over vanilla ice cream. Choose only uniformly shaped, unblemished plums for this dish. The fruit must be left whole, otherwise the flesh will cloud the brandy.

1 bottle Brandy, 26-ounce size

1 cup sugar

1 quart whole purple plums

Combine brandy and sugar, stirring until sugar is dissolved. Pack washed, unblemished plums into sterilized quart jars. Pour brandy mixture over fruit, covering completely. Seal and let stand in a cool dark place for at least 2 months.

Yields 2 quarts.

*Plums Macerated in Brandy served by ▶
innkeeper Darlene Peerless of Wickwire House, Kentville, NS*

POACHED PEACHES WITH VANILLA CREME

DALVAY-BY-THE-SEA, DALVAY, PEI

*Chef Keith Wilson presents this desert with molded Pistachio Wafers. He prepares
the Vanilla Creme using a vanilla bean, but for the ease of the home cook,
I have adjusted the recipe to use vanilla extract.*

3 cups sugar

4 cups water

1 cinnamon stick

1 bay leaf

4 large peaches, ripe but firm

Vanilla Creme, recipe follows

2 tablespoons chopped pistachio nuts,
as garnish

Combine sugar, water, cinnamon and bay leaf
in a deep pot and boil 3 minutes to form a
medium syrup.

Lightly cut a cross in the top of each peach
and gently lower them into the simmering
syrup. The peaches should be completely
submerged. Poach for 3 minutes. Remove
saucepan from heat and allow peaches to cool,
still covered in the syrup. Remove cinnamon
stick and bay leaf.

To assemble desserts, remove peaches from
cooled syrup and gently peel off the skins.

Spread a small circle of vanilla cream on each
serving plate, top with a peach. Sprinkle with
pistachio nuts.

Serves 4.

Vanilla Creme

1 cup heavy cream (35% m.f.)

3 tablespoons sugar

5 large eggs, separated

1/2 teaspoon vanilla

Place cream in a saucepan and bring to a
simmer over low heat. Whisk sugar and yolks
together in a small bowl until creamy, then
gently pour hot cream into egg mixture and
stir well. Place in a double boiler over
simmering water and cook, stirring constantly
until the consistency of thick custard. Remove
from heat, stir in vanilla and whisk over ice
until cool. Place plastic wrap over the surface
of custard to prevent a skin from forming and
refrigerate until set.

*Poached Peaches with Vanilla Creme as served in the inviting dining room of ▶
Dalvay-by-the-Sea, Dalvay, PEI*

INDEX